Endorsements

"Artificial intelligence? Sure. But *people intelligence comes first.* Machine learning? Of course. But *people learning* comes first. Why? Because *people first* is the bedrock of all sustainable endeavors for any enterprise. At a time when we are all getting slapped in the face in ways that isolate us from one another, we need to recommit to values that reconnect us. John's *People First* book shows us how we can do so. It is a must-read for our times."

~ Geoffrey Moore, Author of *Crossing the Chasm* and *Zone to Win*

"As long as I've known John Philpin, since the early days at Oracle, he has been practicing People First leadership. I was an early-in-career inside sales leader, and he was a C-level executive. The fact that he paid any attention to me at all when I didn't even report to him demonstrates his lifelong dedication to a new way of doing business. In this book, John treats us to a thorough exploration of his philosophy, as well as specific ways to put it into action. Not only will this lead you to achieve greater results, but this also positions you to create a richer, more enjoyable workplace culture."

~ Anneke Seley, Co-author of *Sales 2.0* and *Next Era Selling*

"John is as generous as it gets. He is giving away much wisdom, written in his easy and accessible style, that you will not notice how many pages you read in a sitting. It's all so relevant, so true, and so useful. You will finish this excellent book really quickly and keep returning to it as you put so much of it into practice."

~ Rene Carayol, MBE

"In *People First*, John Philpin recognizes and draws our attention to the powerful idea that, when business leaders put people first in their thinking, their businesses will shape (or reshape) themselves into much more powerful entities. Most of us know this is harder to do than to think about. John has distilled and invigorated some key points essential to this task."

~ Mary Ann Allison, MBA, PhD, Co-author of *New Media, Communication, and Society* and *The Complexity Advantage*

"John carefully considers problems from different perspectives, lenses, and disciplines and diverse cultural possibilities. He is able to create a range of possible solutions to give an idea every opportunity to be successful. This is one of his many critical strengths, which makes him fantastic and energetic to partner with. The world will now get a look at this professional wisdom fortunately captured in this book. This book will now help others consider the principles inside that are required to be a 21st-century leader in consideration of sustainable and meaningful healthy possibilities."

~ Daniel Szuc, Keynote Presenter, Consultant, and Author of *Global UX*

"I've always believed that value is in the 'I' of the beholder. Value, it's personal. I've always seen value discussed in a transactional context, but what John's book does is shine a light on the human side of it, a People First paradigm. This shifts the idea of value into its purest form. To value others as people, all-inclusive— their personhood, their ideas, their lives, their beliefs. This could not be a more relevant concept for leaders today, as the tide is shifting to a more human-centric view of business, either within the organizational dynamic or how an organization interacts with society. John's book offers key frameworks and ideas on how to embody the essential tenets of value and make them a reality."

~ Cristina DiGiacomo, Practical Philosopher, and Best-selling Author of *Wise Up! At Work*

"At a time when so many are asking, "Now what?", John is reminding us of a single rule: get (and stay) engaged. For those unsure how exactly to get started, here's a hint: buy a copy of his book for a colleague, read it with them, then discuss and debate each theorem and corollary. As my twenty-plus-year friendship with John has proven, there is great value in the thoughtful exchange of ideas that comes from a nourished connection."

~ Stuart Robbins, Author of *The System Is the Mirror*

"The ESG metrics created by the World Economic Forum's International Business Council in 2020 are structured on four pillars: the Principles of Governance, the Planet, People, and Prosperity. The metrics aim to enable companies to collectively report nonfinancial disclosures and put focus onto quality of life.

"No matter how technology evolves, we need people. So, these people need to be motivated and valued by many means, be that stakeholder engagement, ethical behaviour, taking action on climate change, being able to fulfill their potential in dignity and equality, or knowing that they can enjoy prosperous and fulfilling lives and that economic, social, and technological progress occurs in harmony with nature. These are the kinds of things that people value, but even more so after the pandemic experience. Action is needed now.

"John's message is clear and strong: create value for your people now, then they will create value with your customers. In a world desperately short of talent, it would be a foolish leader who did not pay attention to John's lessons."
~ Dominic Rowsell, Author of *Why Killer Products Don't Sell*

"Customers have always occupied markets. But they didn't run them until they became equipped for exactly that in our new digital age. Problem is, companies—in marketing, especially—typically imagine that they can still 'target,' 'acquire,' 'control,' 'manage,' and 'lock in' customers as if they were serfs in corporate castles. That imaginary world ends when companies get slapped in the face by customer independence, agency, originality, resourcefulness, and other abilities that were limited or prevented in industrial times. Among those formerly repressed powers are new ways to reach out, to help, and to improve what companies are and can do in our new digital world. These facts are among many that John Philpin knows better than nearly every other source of insight you can find—and that's why you need this book."
~ Doc Searls, Author of *The Intention Economy: When Customers Take Charge* and Co-author of *The Cluetrain Manifesto*

When we least expect it, we can all be slapped in the face. I've recently been slapped myself and have applied this methodology to my personal situation.

Get the worksheet that would allow you to apply this methodology to transform, transition, and transcend your situation by going to:
https://peoplefirst.business/connect/read-your-book

FOR BUSINESS LEADERS SLAPPED IN THE FACE BY A WORLD THEY THOUGHT THEY KNEW

A HUMAN'S GUIDE TO OUR NEW WORLD — AND HOW TO MAKE IT WORK FOR US

John Philpin

Foreword by
Stuart A. Robbins

THiNKaha®

An Actionable Business Journal

E-mail: info@thinkaha.com
20660 Stevens Creek Blvd., Suite 210
Cupertino, CA 95014

Please go to
https://aha.pub/SlapInTheFace
to read this AHAbook and to share the
individual AHA messages that resonate with you.

*AHA*that·

Published by THiNKaha®
20660 Stevens Creek Blvd., Suite 210,
Cupertino, CA 95014
https://thinkaha.com
E-mail: info@thinkaha.com

THiNK*aha*®

First Printing: August 2021
Hardcover ISBN: 978-1-61699-387-0   1-61699-387-1
Paperback ISBN: 978-1-61699-386-3   1-61699-386-3
eBook ISBN: 978-1-61699-385-6   1-61699-385-5
Place of Publication: Silicon Valley, California, USA
Paperback Library of Congress Number: 2020922892

Images used in the cover and book sections are from gapingvoid®

Dedication

For Isla-Mae and Everly.

In the hope that you both grow into a world that is worthy of you.

If we all take these lessons, learn from them, and apply them, surely all our grandchildren will grow into a better world than the one they were born into?

Acknowledgements

There is only one name on this book, but many people have made it possible: my friends, family, colleagues, business partners, mentors, managers, teams over the years, customers, competitors, the people I meet who share their stories, the People First community, acquaintances, etc. Even those I have disagreed with—everything is a lesson.

Thank you—all of you. Each of you has influenced who I am and the story I am sharing. Without you all, there is no People First.

My book includes a short biography, and you will see that I have spent a career in the business of software. If you check the various people who have said nice things about me and the book, you will see that they, too, are primarily from the software business.

But this book is not about software nor even technology. It is about people. It is about you. With that, my particular thanks to:

Stuart Robbins, who keeps me honest, real, and focused and was kind enough to write a foreword for this book.

Laura Viberti, Jason Korman, and Hugh Macleod at **Gaping Void** for working with me to make the images work throughout the book.

Mitchell Levy, Jenilee Maniti, Nikka Ann Alejandro, and the rest of the team at **THiNKaha** for doing everything else!

A THiNKaha book is not your typical book. It's a whole lot more while being a whole lot less. Scan the QR code or use this link to watch me talk about this new evolutionary style of book: https://aha.pub/THiNKahaSeries

How to Read a THiNKaha® Book

A Note from the Publisher

The AHAthat/THiNKaha series was crafted to deliver content the way humans process information in today's world. Short, sweet, and to the point while delivering powerful, lasting impact.

The content is designed and presented in ways to appeal to visual, auditory, and kinesthetic personality types. Each section contains AHA messages, lines for notes, and a meme that summarizes that section. You should also scan the QR code, or click on the link, to watch a video of the author talking about that section.

This book is contextual in nature. Although the words won't change, their meaning will every time you read it as your context will. Be ready, you will experience your own AHA moments as you read. The AHA messages are designed to be stand-alone actionable messages that will help you think differently. Items to consider as you're reading include:

1. It should only take less than an hour to read the first time. When you're reading, write one to three action items that resonate with you in the underlined areas.
2. Mark your calendar to re-read it again.
3. Repeat step #1 and mark one to three additional AHA messages that resonate. As they will most likely be different, this is a great time to reflect on the messages that resonated with you during your last reading.
4. Sprinkle credust on the author and yourself by sharing the AHA messages from this book socially from the AHAthat platform https://aha.pub/SlapInTheFace.

After reading this THiNKaha book, marking your AHA messages, rereading it, and marking more AHA messages, you'll begin to see how this book contextually applies to you. We advocate for continuous, lifelong learning and this book will help you transform your AHAs into action items with tangible results.

Mitchell Levy, Global Credibility Expert
publisher@thinkaha.com

THiNKaha®

Contents

This is the Table of Contents (TOC) from the book for your reference.

An Introduction to People First

I have been writing this book all my life. I've included versions of it in sales pitches I've delivered, presentations I've made, and conversations I've had. The lessons are definitely part of the many 'change' programs that I have been a part of. While the methods I talk about are tried and tested, the difference is that I have transformed them into ideas that can be adopted by anyone, without the need for the support of a multi-national conglomerate.

It's clear that no matter what you think that you might know, you can always learn more. By applying the lessons of this book, you will come to understand how to work with the world on your own terms—not someone else's.

I started developing the ideas behind People First when I stopped being a full-time member of the 'corporate world.' It took a while to settle into the groove, but my passion drove me because I knew I was onto something. With each day, it became clearer that this was my purpose. When I first sat down and developed the original concept, tenets, and frameworks of this thinking, I used the term, 'People Power.'

As you read this book and work through the '3T journey', you will learn the importance of the people around you. Understand who they are, listen to them, and act accordingly. That's exactly what I did. That's why the initiative is called People First, not People Power.

A topic as substantial as one about people can't avoid politics, albeit spelt with a small 'p.' Culture, religion, war, social change, equal rights, equal pay are all People First issues but remain outside the scope of this book.

The book is for people—all people—who are (or who aspire to be) in business, specifically business leaders. You might be a small business owner or a team lead in a large corporation. You might be a leader who wants to influence people outside of your 'line responsibility.' You might be just starting out on your journey through life and simply want to work out how you can follow your dreams and passions and make a good living at the same time. Whichever it is, this book is for you.

People First is a state of mind. It is not about 'customer centricity,' 'staff engagement,' or 'equal pay.' It's about you and what you can do to take ownership of your life and position in the spectrum of the world. It is not to be 'centric' or 'focused' or 'lean.' Rather, it is for you to find and define your passion and purpose, to visualize what you want to be and where you want to be in service of that passion and purpose, and to develop a roadmap to take you there with sufficient agility that you can ride the next inevitable wave of change.

This book's focus is business, but not through a different lens or filter nor even standing to one side and seeing it from a different angle. Rather, it seeks to help you view it from a different dimension—to understand an alternative reality, to visualize it, to achieve it.

If you are interested in exploring the foundational thinking of this book a little more deeply, I refer you to the two Appendices at the back of the book.

Foreword by Stuart A. Robbins

Solving the Collaboration Conundrum during Uncertain Times

I first met John in 1999, who was then an executive at a startup called Flypaper, providing web-based collaboration solutions for the Enterprise. I met him again when I launched a knowledge management startup, KMERA (John was Vitria's CMO at the time). Many Silicon Valley clients and companies have come and gone over two decades, and I can honestly say that one of the most valuable keepsakes of those early years has been our twenty-year collegial friendship.

One might describe our relationship as a product of intersecting Silicon Valley careers and shared philosophies. While it's true that we have 'software development' in our background, this Foreword reflects a broader, multi-faceted connection. Over the years, we have also found ourselves in different geographies, separated by multiple time zones and thousands of miles, and yet even in these uncertain times—when many social/professional connections are suffering prolonged disconnects—we have remained in touch by email and video calls on a weekly basis.

This is John, undeterred by boundaries and barriers, walls, and oceans.

John's pursuit of intellectual clarity in the business community is comparable to those who run into burning buildings to ensure the welfare of the residents while most others would be inclined to run away. Who would dare to write and publish a book of business advice during the greatest series of crises faced by modern man, while most of us are struggling to navigate our daily lives as this maelstrom swirls around us?

This is John, undeterred by the unpredictability and instabilities of life in 2020: looking forward, sharing his observations, and asking that we remain engaged.

Allow me this brief historical reference in order to underscore his courage to embrace the fears that so many others seek to escape.

The Cave-Phantom Myth

Seventeen thousand years ago in the south of France, there was a significant transition in our development. It was a behavioral shift, overlooked until 1940, when a young boy's dog named Robot fell into a hole. While rescuing Robot, the boy discovered the Lascaux Caves[1], with walls covered by more than 600 cave paintings—one of the earliest known examples of prehistoric art and now a World Heritage Site.

Let me put the cave paintings into context. Humans had just realized the benefit (safety from weather, predators, etc.) of cave dwellings, with one unexpected element of fires for warmth and caves for security: flickering shadows on the wall believed to be mountain spirits. They quickly learned that the spirits became even larger when someone moved away from them, which caused even more fear until a generation later, when it was also learned that the spirits grew smaller when approached, because they were shadows caused by the light of the fires.

By confronting the myth of cave phantoms, not only did social fears of unseen spirits diminish, but the knowledge also allowed them to begin expressing themselves by painting shapes of animals throughout the cave, paintings that have remained to this day.

Many of us would benefit from re-learning the value of facing the source of our anxieties, particularly in business during times of uncertainty. (We have an aversion to the flickering unknown that seems to be getting larger even as we pull back.) More to the point, there's this well-known but rarely admitted challenge in the tech community: if you were to ask, as I have done, a community of CIOs and CTOs what's their single greatest worry, they will rarely identify technical issues. This is because most technology problems, with sufficient time and financing, can be solved. The greatest challenge for most IT executives is people.

---

[1]For more info about the cave paintings, see: https://en.wikipedia.org/wiki/Lascaux.

Our managers are not trained to manage people (and many chose a technology career because they'd prefer to avoid those challenges). Our teams are often dysfunctional. No one talks to each other—perhaps because no one has been trained to listen.

John is setting an alternate example with People First. He's focused on these core issues at a time when concurrent problems are swirling around every type of business—large, small, and medium-sized—and around every family and community organization by reminding us that these problems are cave phantoms.

At a time when so many are asking, 'Now what?' John is reminding us of a single rule: get and stay engaged.

For those unsure how, exactly, to get started, here's a hint: buy a copy of his book for a colleague, read it with them, then discuss and debate each stage. As my twenty-year friendship with John has proven, there is great value in the thoughtful exchange of ideas that comes from a nourished connection.

Concluding Thoughts

Those who have followed John's newsletter, blog, and podcast will recognize a solid foundation in modern technology theory—from a recognition that 'value' in an information-based economy increases when it is shared (network economics) to second-generation cybernetics, which spans the spectrum of network theory from the work of Teilhard de Chardin to modern economic models embedded in sophisticated IT architectures.

People First is more than a human resources concept and more than an organizational development theme. Rather, it is a fundamental rule for anyone involved in the design and development of technology and beyond—though aren't we all technology companies in 2020?

People First is a business framework in complete harmony with the Prime Theorem of my 2007 book, *Lessons in Grid Computing: The System Is a Mirror*[2].

---

[2] New York: John Wiley & Sons

It states that information systems mirror the organizations that design and build them. (This is the solution to every tech company's frustration when replacing a legacy system with something new, only to discover old problems re-surfacing upon rollout.) The metaphor is simple: imagine that you are standing in front of a full-length mirror, unhappy with what you see. Rather than adopting a healthier diet, you solve the problem by replacing the mirror.

There are obvious corollaries: to correct the flaws in our information systems, we must therefore correct the flaws in the teams and organizations supporting those systems. As one of my colleagues in the semi-conductor industry often said:

> "Our systems will not talk to each other if the people are not talking to each other."

In summary:

We cannot transform our systems until we transform ourselves.

We are nodes in the network upon which all commerce proceeds.

We are the platform upon which our inter-connected businesses thrive.

This is much more than a socio-psychological catch phrase—it is a central principle for the architectural resilience and viability of our information systems in the twenty-first century.

Particularly in these uncertain times, People First answers the big question: now what? It offers an architectural concept upon which your transformed business must exist in order to thrive. It is the secret to success in a networked, information-based economy.

Stuart A. Robbins
December 2020

Share the AHA messages from this book socially by going to
https://aha.pub/SlapInTheFace.

Scan the QR code or use this link to watch the section videos and more on this section topic:
https://aha.pub/SlapInTheFaceSVs

Section I

Your World Has Changed

'Expect the unexpected' has been part of our lexicon for generations. It is so ingrained in our psyche that we forget about it. When it happened, we froze.

Life is not what it was, and if we're careful, we're not going back. The world changes so fast that it significantly outpaces everyone's expectations. This is no blip on the radar. When things go back to 'normal', what do you think that 'normal' will be? What do you think it should be?

Nobody is exempt. Change has affected every human on the planet. It has flipped businesses upside down and destroyed others. Business leaders find themselves slapped in the face by a world they thought they knew.

It's not as if business leaders didn't have enough time to see what might have been coming; it's just that they've been caught out by the speed of the occurrence. Years of our future have been compressed into a couple of financial quarters because of change.

1

Business leaders have been slapped in the face by a world they thought they knew. To succeed in our #ChangingWorld they need to change — and keep changing.

_____

_____

_____

2

Life and business is not what it was. It's not going back. The world is changing in a way that has significantly outpaced many people's expectations. Some business leaders are not able to keep up with this #ChangingWorld.

_____

_____

_____

3

Change is given. And now, so is the the speed of change. The accelerating rate of change is the #NewNormal. Can business leaders keep up?

_____

_____

_____

4

Business leaders had plenty of time to see the #Change coming. But when it came, they froze. Slapped in the face by a world they thought they knew, they did not expect the unexpected. How prepared are you in the face of change?

_____

_____

_____

5

#Change raises warning signs everywhere. Business leaders need to pay attention because change happens at hyperbolic speed.

_____

_____

_____

6

#Change is two-faced. If you implement change, it is good. If change is applied to you, it is not. It is crucial to get ahead of the curve, and to be proactive with change!

_____

_____

_____

7

#Change IS scary. It carries uncertainty. No one can predict what happens next, that's up to you! It's important to be prepared to navigate through change.

_____

_____

_____

8

The world has #Changed. That isn't the surprise. It is constantly changing. It will not be the same again. Business leaders can mitigate this change if they are prepared. How prepared are you to adapt to change?

_____

_____

_____

9

It's tough to make predictions, especially about the future.
#Change — Yogi Berra

10

#Change is happening to every business leader.
Nobody is exempt. Change has affected every human
on the planet. It's flipped businesses upside down and
destroyed others.

---

a transformative mindset is:

competence
confidence
courage

@gapingvoid

Share the AHA messages from this book socially by going to
https://aha.pub/SlapInTheFace.

Scan the QR code or use this link to watch the
section videos and more on this section topic:
https://aha.pub/SlapInTheFaceSVs

Section II

You Need to Transform to Change

Controlled change over time is never easy but can be mitigated if you control the change in your own time. The change in 2020 was different, unprecedented. It happened globally and affected every tier of society, every country, and every business. Things that we took to be normal on the eve of 2020 might not return until 2025. Are you ready for that?

Businesses need to adapt, morph, and change—or will likely cease to exist.

A business's success *and* failure lies with the leader. They need to acknowledge that today's world is different than yesterday's. They know that for their business to succeed, they need to personally succeed. What they might not yet have come to terms with is that for their business to succeed, every stakeholder in their business needs to succeed. Success is not impossible to achieve, but a personal transformation is required in order to face change.

The level of vision and courage of people in a business differentiates the businesses that succeed and those that don't.

11

Business leaders have been slapped in the face by a world they thought they knew. It's not stopping. It's not even slowing down. It's accelerating. You either #Change or cease to exist.

_____

_____

_____

12

An accelerated #Change in this world has been predicted for years. Business leaders who acknowledge this are prepared to keep up. The rest will cease to exist. How can you keep pace with this accelerated change?

_____

_____

_____

13

The illiterate of the 21st century will not be those who cannot read and write, but those who cannot learn, unlearn, and relearn. #Change — Pablo Picasso

_____

_____

_____

14

#Change or don't. It's your choice. Much like survival, when you are threatened, you just don't accept it, you fight and you win by outsmarting the opposition. Agility is your friend. Are you agile enough to win?

_____

_____

_____

15

It takes vision to stay ahead of the curve. You chart your course, plan for the roadblocks, and set sail. What is your vision? #NeedToChange

_____

_____

_____

16

Business leaders need to understand their business, and to do that, they need to understand the people in their posse. Who's in your posse? #Change

_____

_____

_____

17

A business's success and failure lies with the leader. They need to acknowledge that today's world is different than yesterday's. In order for their business to succeed, they need to succeed. #Change

_____

_____

_____

18

Success is not impossible to achieve. One just needs to undergo a personal transformation in order to face #Change and succeed.

_____

_____

_____

19

To survive in the new world, some businesses automate, manufacture offshore, and outsource jobs. What do you need to #Change for your business to continue to exist?

20

The level of vision and the courage of people in a business differentiate the businesses that succeed and those that don't. #NeedToChange

---

21

Business leaders have the wisdom to focus on controlling that which they can control. By focusing on the span of control within their sphere, their businesses will succeed. #Change

_____

_____

_____

22

The world has changed. It's going to keep changing. Business leaders need to ride that wave of change, adapt themselves, and be ready when it breaks. #Success #Survival

_____

_____

_____

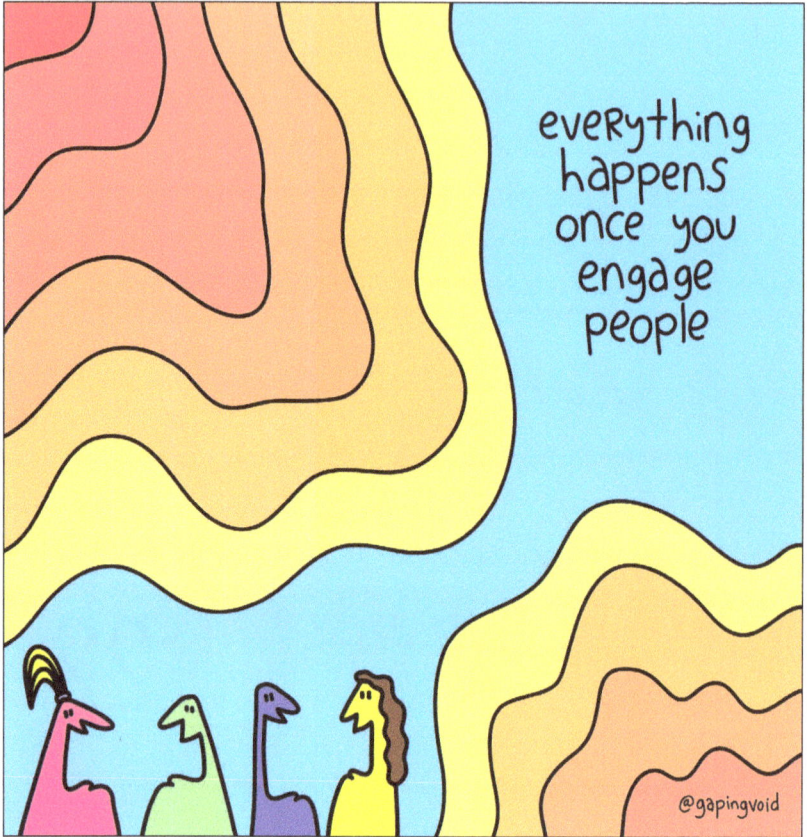

Share the AHA messages from this book socially by going to
https://aha.pub/SlapInTheFace.

*Scan the QR code or use this link to watch the
section videos and more on this section topic:*
https://aha.pub/SlapInTheFaceSVs

Section III

Putting People First Is the Key to Success

In recent years, businesses have become so preoccupied with profit, growth, and scale, they have forgotten that people come first.

In a rapidly changing world, understanding the value of human connection is one of the key things needed for businesses to succeed. They need to know who their customers are and whom they're working with.

Human connection requires trust.

The push-style promotion and sales of products and service have been under threat for many years. The need for businesses and their staff to know their customers, engage with them, converse with them, and support them is once more top of mind. Then, and only then, can businesses start to develop trusted relationships.

Business leaders need stakeholders in their staff. Employees need to feel like they are part of the business as much as the leader is. If everyone has a stake in the company, they will make sure it will survive and thrive in a constantly changing world.

A **People First** business has a solid foundation and will survive and thrive in our ever-changing world.

23

People FIRST: Understand the ENTIRE team. Process SECOND: What resources do you have to achieve your goals? Then, and only then, do we start to think about the technology needed to create a successful business. #Change

_____

_____

_____

24

The world seems to have gotten businesses away from the human connection. They now use CRMs and email systems. Technology provides a platform, but people need to be placed first for businesses to succeed. #Change

---

25

Many businesses are too preoccupied with accelerating their growth and scaling. They implement and walk away. They forget that people should come first. This will set them up for failure in the new world. #Change

---

26

When in possession of an absolutely brilliant service that already exists, business leaders can combine human connection and technology. This will bring on their winning game. #Change

_____

_____

_____

27

Understanding that people come first is one of the key things for businesses to succeed. How well do you know the people in your community? #Change

_____

_____

_____

28

Social selling is what business leaders use to succeed in business today. To keep up with a changing world, it's all about returning selling to where it was years ago. It's about knowing the people you are talking to. #Change

_____

_____

_____

29

Business leaders need to know who their customers are and whom they work with (their employees and partners). Understanding the people around them is key to understanding the market they serve. #Change

_____

_____

_____

30

Businesses that survive #Change are those that build relationships with their customers. They fight to stay afloat in their own way to service customers and keep their loyalty.

31

Business leaders can retain their competitive edge through human connection. Building a loyal customer and partner base ensures the continuity of their business. #Change

---

32

Emotional connection is powerful! Business leaders who can emotionally connect with their customers will attract a huge following. How do you keep your customers engaged? #Change

---

33

Business leaders who have the courage to tell their story make themselves relatable to people. People will want to buy from them because they like the person behind the business. #Change

---

34

Business moves at the speed of trust. Getting to know customers, conversing with them, and giving them support wins that trust. Win the trust and people will support you. #Change

_____

_____

_____

35

In the new world, employee experience is just as valuable as customer experience. Improving the quality of the work you need done will ensure that the business retains its best talent. #Change

_____

_____

_____

36

A positive employee experience will set a business up for success in our new world. Business leaders need to think about all of their employees. How can you create a positive experience for your employees? #Change

_____

_____

_____

37

The people who are crazy enough to think they can #Change the world are the ones who do. — Steve Jobs

_____

_____

_____

38

Transparency toward stakeholders is critical. If everyone sees the picture, they become more efficient contributors to the business. How can you promote transparency in your business? #Change

_____

_____

_____

39

Life consists mostly of sleep, family, and work. Business leaders can help improve the quality of their employees' lives by considering these factors, and in return, the business will benefit from increased engagement. #Change

_____

_____

_____

40

The new world sees the movement from shareholder value to stakeholder value. The real sharing economy is where all stakeholders benefit and rise with the tide. Are your employees stakeholders in your business? How? #Change

_____

_____

_____

41

Different stakeholders have different needs. Business leaders will need to take a different approach or solution for each stakeholder. Once needs are addressed, business success improves. #Change

_____

_____

_____

42

Business leaders stand to gain if their employees grow together with their customers. Everyone becomes a stakeholder in the business's success. #Change

_____

_____

_____

43

A business can greatly benefit if the people who run it are stakeholders. If they do a good job, everyone in the business, as well as the business itself, stands to succeed. #Change

_____

_____

_____

44

Employees need to feel like they are part of the business as much as the leader is. If everyone has a stake in the company, they will make sure the business survives and thrives in a constantly changing world. #Change

_____

_____

_____

45

Business leaders need to think of ways that their employees can do things more quickly and make them feel better about doing their job. This raises stakeholder value and positively impacts the business's success. #Change

---

46

Employees who are involved in a #Transition plan need to own the plan and the vision. Their commitment to the transition and the business is stronger because they are part of it.

47

People are searching for engagement. Human Connection engages people. Business leaders who put people first stand to succeed in our new world. #Change

_____

_____

_____

48

Business leaders need to think about their business holistically. They need to think of what they can do for everyone who is part of it. This ensures that people will want to work with them and buy from their business. #Change

_____

_____

_____

to add value to others

one must first value others

@gapingvoid

Share the AHA messages from this book socially by going to
https://aha.pub/SlapInTheFace.

Scan the QR code or use this link to watch the section videos and more on this section topic:
https://aha.pub/SlapInTheFaceSVs

Section IV

If People Are the Key, Value Is the Lock

Understanding this is essential for all business leaders to thrive in an ever-changing world with the new contract. Value is the lock that's guarding the new contract.

Of course, it is easy to assume that if your business has not been affected, you are impervious to these problems. Never underestimate luck. This time, you might have been lucky. What about next time? What does your plan say? A business that has been strong for decades does not have any guarantee that they will continue to be strong in the future.

There is a good reason that financial services use the standard disclaimer clause in their advertising:

"Past success does not guarantee future performance."

We know that but we still don't pay attention. It's as if we need to be slapped in the face by a world we thought we knew to even sit up and pay attention!

Value provides a needed lock on survival and transcendence. But be careful about that word.

Traditional thinking will tell you that customers are willing to pay more for better quality and experience, and businesses can reap huge profits by understanding what their customers value.

Traditional thinking will tell you that employees are willing to work harder and smarter if they feel 'valued' by the company they work for. Employee retention programs will tell you that having a positive working experience can motivate your staff to help the business succeed. If leaders can find ways to serve more people and provide value, their businesses will grow in an expanding market. Adding value to the community attracts their loyalty and ensures the survival of a business in a world that is in constant change.

But that's only part of the story.

Value is a word that twists in the wind. It is often associated with monetary worth, but the nuances of value are far more sophisticated. Value, like beauty, is in the eye of the beholder. Context, available resources, history, needs, wants, timing, luck, and knowledge are just pieces of a whole set of variables that contribute to the final 'value', which will vary from person to person, over time, and across geographies.

In other words, *value is not absolute.* Value is measured at that moment in time by both parties, under a specific context, in a specific location.

Value, once understood, will change your world.

Trust, humanity, connection, truth, honesty, and transparency are just a few of the factors that every single stakeholder has to understand to accept the new contract for the new world.

That's value.

49

#Value is what people perceive to be important to them. People are the key. Value is the lock that a business needs to succeed in our changing world.

_____

_____

_____

50

Just because companies have been doing well for decades does not mean they will continue to exist in the future. Only businesses that add #Value, customer by customer, will thrive and so, survive.

_____

_____

_____

51

Our old world saw structure and categorization as the route to success. Business leaders now need to think about adding #Value when doing business. Value is the lock. The world has #Changed.

_____

_____

_____

52

#Value is in the eye of the beholder. Value depends on the situation, the person, and the context. Business leaders will benefit from adding unique and differentiated value in every situation.

_____

_____

_____

53

Business leaders should ask themselves how they can improve the quality of time of their customers, employees, and partners. What are the ways of improving the quality of time of the people in your sphere? #Value

_____

_____

_____

54

Managing company reputation is hard. Reputation is built on the #Value that the market perceives it to have. Business leaders need to focus on increasing the value of their business.

_____

_____

_____

55

Businesses are struggling because they are measuring the wrong things. Business leaders need to find and use things that are important to people and match their #Value.

_____

_____

_____

56

Business leaders need to identify where their market potential is. What #Value can their businesses offer to tap into that target market share?

_____

_____

_____

57

Knowing one's customer can shape the processes of designing and developing products that will sell. It helps business leaders identify what brings #Value to their market.

_____

_____

_____

58

Customers are willing to pay more for better quality and experience. Businesses need to understand what their customers #Value. How well do you understand what your customers value?

_____

_____

_____

59

When business leaders understand why customers come to them, they understand the #Value their businesses have. Only then can they leverage this to increase value in other markets.

_____

_____

_____

60

If business leaders can find ways to serve more people, their businesses can add more #Value. Businesses that add value can continue to exist in our new world. How can you serve more people?

_____

_____

_____

61

A holistic way of doing business is key to succeeding in our new world. It's all about adding #Value not only to customers but to employees as well. How can you add value to both your customers and employees?

_____

_____

_____

62

Companies need to understand the #Value of the people in their organization. People are the key — their value is the lock. How can you put your people first?

_____

_____

_____

63

Business leaders need to understand their 'assets under management' and work to translate those assets into something of #Value. This is the future of business.

_____

_____

_____

64

Wealth is made by well-managed asset utilization, not by the time spent working on a job. This is the future of income, not work. #Value

_____

_____

_____

65

A wealthy person does not make their money by working on a job. They leverage their assets to make money. What assets can you potentially leverage to make money? #Value

_____

_____

_____

66

There is no future of work. Transactional work is increasingly delivered by machines. Business leaders need to shift their thinking to the future of income. #Value

_____

_____

_____

67

The future of income is based on leveraging assets to create #Value. Value will change depending on whom a business leader is dealing with. How can you leverage your assets to create value for the people around you?

_____

_____

_____

68

#Value is not about measuring time. It is about measuring worth. Business leaders need to measure their employees by the value they bring to the business.

_____

_____

_____

69

Paying someone for the #Value they give to the business could potentially save business leaders more time. What are the ways you can save more of your time?

_____

_____

_____

70

Business leaders need to think in terms of #Value and not time. In dealing with employees, they need to start thinking about paying them by value and not by time. How can you make this shift from time to value?

_____

_____

_____

71

Employees become engaged when the quality of their employee experience increases. Businesses will grow when their employees feel #Valued. What are the ways you can make your employees feel valued?

_____

_____

_____

72

#Value is always in the eye of the beholder.
— Jonathan Heller

_____

_____

_____

73

Focus on providing #Value to both customers and employees, and the businesses will receive value in return.

_____

_____

_____

74

Delivering #Value is so important that business leaders will benefit from going to their community and asking how they can add value for them. How can you add value to your community?

_____

_____

_____

75

Business leaders need to think in terms of #Value. Value is critical for businesses to survive and thrive in a constantly changing world.

_____

_____

_____

plan in decades

think in years

work in months

live
in
days

@gapingvoid

Share the AHA messages from this book socially by going to
https://aha.pub/SlapInTheFace.

*Scan the QR code or use this link to watch the
section videos and more on this section topic:*
https://aha.pub/SlapInTheFaceSVs

Section V

Plan to Transform—to Transition

The world may have changed forever. You need to change, but not forever. You need to change and then change again. It's a different way of thinking. You need to leave your comfort zone behind. Again and again and again. This starts with personal transformation.

Transformation allows people to start the journey of transition, a fundamental building block to managing change.

Transition requires a five-step plan that takes you through a process of discovery, design, decision, development, and deployment.

The first two phases, discovery and design, will allow you to set up your transition plan.

Discover

Discovery is a journey that explores your 'current reality' and seeks to connect it to your 'future vision.' You need to figure out the current state of the business, the marketplace it's in, and the world it's operating in. Be honest with yourself. The world won't care and nor should you. It just slapped you in the face—it's time to fight back.

A journey by yourself is lonely, so make sure you take people with you. Talk to your customers and colleagues, and learn from other businesses and what they are doing. Outside competitors will benefit from going through the discovery process with the people around them. The more brains involved, the better the plan will be.

Design

Designing a transition plan requires mapping it backward from the end goal. Leaders need to prioritize the order of things. This is where they can benefit from having their community involved in setting up their transition plan.

After that, it will be easier for them to handle change and successfully navigate through it.

76

The world has changed. Business leaders need to #Transition to keep up with the change. Having a transition plan can help leaders prepare their businesses to survive and thrive change.

_____

_____

_____

77

The current reality of business leaders is they've just been slapped in the face by a world that isn't what they knew. The world is no longer what they thought it was. #Transition

_____

_____

_____

78

Transitioning requires a well-mapped-out plan. There are two phases of the transition plan: #Discovery and #Design. #Transition

_____

_____

_____

79

A transition plan requires #Discovery. Business leaders need to figure out where their businesses stand in this new world.

_____

_____

_____

80

The journey of #Discovery is connecting current reality to future vision. How can you connect your current reality to your future vision?

_____

_____

_____

81

Business leaders need to write down everything about their current reality. It may be difficult, but they have to be honest and truthful about it. #Discovery

_____

_____

_____

82

Business leaders need to write down what their future vision is. What do they want to do? Where do they want their business to go? Then they need to validate the reality with their community. #Discovery

_____

_____

_____

83

Business leaders need to decide on a timeframe
that suits the transition plan for their business.
Their community will help them plan the time table.
#Discovery

_____

_____

_____

84

The #Discovery process includes finding and
understanding data that will be used to make a sound
transition plan.

_____

_____

_____

85

An inventory of assets is an important list that business leaders need to come up with. These assets are going to be utilized in that roadmap of getting from point A to B. #Discovery

---

86

Documentation is a critical part of #Discovery. Write it all down. Everything. There is no uncertainty when it is written. It clarifies.

87

Business leaders need to identify what assets they do not have that are necessary for their #Transition plan. How do you overcome the lack of these assets?

_____

_____

_____

88

Benchmarking thriving businesses is a great way for business leaders to learn to adapt. They will find the answers by asking how modern-day businesses operate.

_____

_____

_____

89

Business leaders will benefit from the #Discovery process by involving the people around them. The more brains involved, the better the transition plan will turn out to be.

_____

_____

_____

90

It does not do to leave a live dragon out of your calculations, if you live near one. #Discovery
— J.R.R. Tolkien

_____

_____

_____

91

The second step in the transition plan is #Design.
Best approach? Start looking backward. Business
leaders should reverse back from their end goal.

_____

_____

_____

92

A #Transition plan requires laying out the roadmap that
gets you from here to there. This is the roadmap for
business leaders to transition their businesses in this
changing world.

_____

_____

_____

93

In #Designing a transition plan for their business, leaders will notice that some things connect and other things will be parallel to each other. This will help them see where the adjustments need to be made.

_____

_____

_____

94

In mapping out a transition plan, business leaders are going to hit certain trip points on the journey. Enter iteration: What are the possible roadblocks in your #Transition plan? #Design

---

95

Inspiration is a key element in #Designing a transition plan. Business leaders need to prioritize the order of things. This is where they need to listen to what their gut says.

96

Part of setting up a #Transition plan is having some form of community. Business leaders can benefit from having the community of those people they might serve be involved.

_____

_____

_____

97

Business leaders need their people around to be part of that community that will help them set up their #Transition plan. There will be different perspectives and one common goal. Who is part of your community?

_____

_____

_____

98

When #Designing their transition plan, business leaders and their team need to brainstorm. Listing the pros and cons of each of the potential routes they could take happens here.

_____

_____

_____

99

As people go through the cycle of change, they experience a full range of things. Setting up the #Transition plan is a critical starting point in this cycle of change.

_____

_____

_____

100

When transitioning to a new world, people move through an emotional rollercoaster. A #Transition plan will help smooth the heart and mind as you look to the changes you are going through.

_____

_____

_____

101

When transitioning to a new world, people go through all kinds of emotional things in moving from point A to B. A #Transition plan will help iron out the changes one is going through.

_____

_____

_____

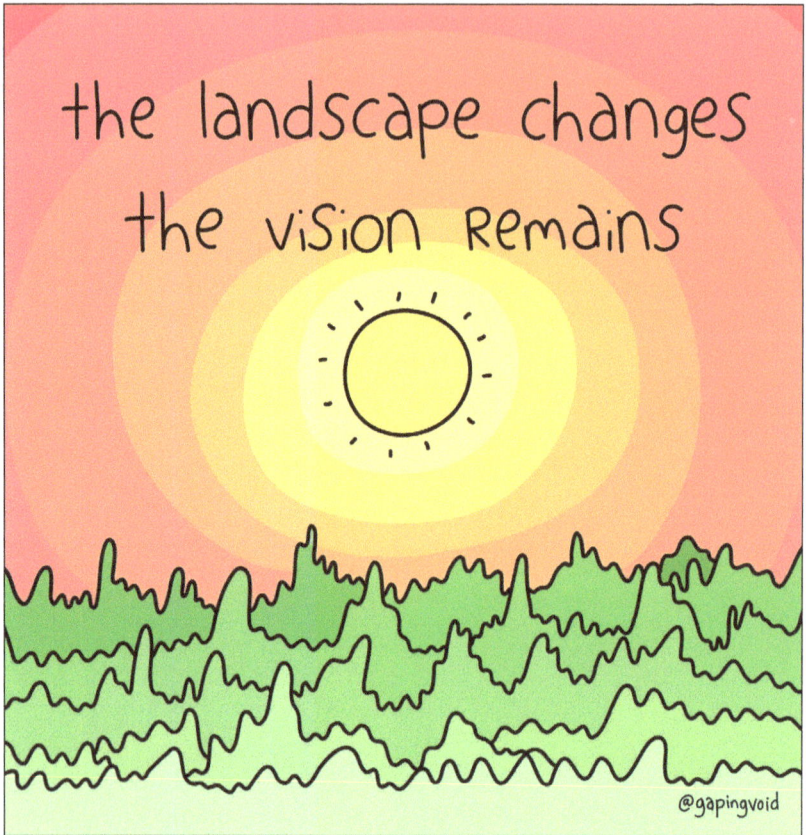

the landscape changes
the vision remains

@gapingvoid

Share the AHA messages from this book socially by going to
https://aha.pub/SlapInTheFace.

Scan the QR code or use this link to watch the section videos and more on this section topic:
https://aha.pub/SlapInTheFaceSVs

Section VI

Plan to Transition—to Transcend

After setting up your transition plan, it's time to make it real.

In the previous section, you came up with a beginning (where you are now) and an end (where you want to be). To get from A to B, there were all kinds of routes you could take, and in the design phase, you detailed them all.

Decide

Decision time: Of all those possible journeys that you explored, which one is the right one to take?

Again, don't do this alone. Journeys are much more fun with others, and there will always be lessons to learn from them. The bigger the community, the more learnings there will be.

During the design process, the entire exercise was one of ideation, releasing all kinds of possibilities that you captured to be explored. Now that reality is kicking in, what can you really do?

A decision on the route is made, and now the details need to be added. In the earlier stages, you might have felt you were looking at a globe in a library. Or imagined that you were on the Space Station, looking down on the world. You couldn't always see outlines of roads, and roadblocks would not have been as clear. That's why you now need a roadmap. It doesn't matter if it's a fold out, an atlas, or on your phone—the important thing is that it is several orders of magnitude more detailed than the globe.

Develop

Potential roadblocks not visible from space will become much clearer on the roadmap.

Remember, a roadblock isn't something that stops you; it's simply something you need to work around.

Working through the process of decision and development is iterative and might result in a feeling of déjà vu. You choose a route and it's working, and then details start to emerge on the roadmap that make you question where you are. You revisit an alternative route from the design stage. You might change. You might merge two different routes. This is fine. All is good. There are no rules, other than the need to go through this process.

Eventually, it all falls into place, and a fully thought-out developed plan is there in front of you. There's only one thing left.

Deployment

The rubber is really hitting the road. We're going to make this real. The good news is that this will be of no surprise to anyone. You've already identified and brought along all the stakeholders within the ecosystem of your business.

102

Multiple roadmaps in a #Transition plan can present business leaders with a veritable raft of options. There is a need to prioritize the better options that will help the business transition in a changing world.

_____

_____

_____

103

In a #Transition plan, there are different roadmaps connecting the current reality with the future vision. Business leaders need to choose the best way they can move forward and succeed in a changing world.

_____

_____

_____

104

#Deciding on the most viable option to transition a business requires mapping the upside and downside of each route to take.

_____

_____

_____

105

#Deciding on a roadmap in a transition plan involves a complex process. Analysis needs to be done. However, business leaders also need to listen to their inner voice. Both are important.

_____

_____

_____

106

When it is obvious that the goals cannot be reached, don't adjust the goals, adjust the action steps. #Decide
— Confucius

_____

_____

_____

107

If a business wants to succeed in our new world, multiple options is not an option. #Decide. #Commit. What is the option you've #Decided on?

_____

_____

_____

108

Business leaders need to #Decide on the roadmap in their transition plan and stick with it. How can you stick with that option you've decided on?

_____

_____

_____

109

Focus allows businesses to go further out and succeed. Businesses that fail don't have the discipline to focus. They entertain too many options. They never say 'no'. #Decide on that one best option.

_____

_____

_____

110

Focus is powerful! Businesses that focus in a specific way succeed. The ones that don't focus do not succeed. #Decide

---

111

Business leaders can work with flexibility when realizing their transition plan. What counts is the decision they #Develop regarding the direction of the business.

112

A transition plan will contain variation. This allows business leaders to shift things around as the #Development of the plan unfolds. How can you prepare for the variations that might occur?

_____

_____

_____

113

There will be obstacles in transitioning a business. With a well #Developed transition plan, it is clear to business leaders how to mitigate such challenges.

_____

_____

_____

114

What is important for business leaders is to work on the transition plan. This is #Deployment. What have you mobilized in transitioning your business?

_____

_____

_____

115

It does not make sense to work on transitioning a business at random. A transition plan is in place for a reason. If business leaders find themselves doing things not in the plan, it means iteration is needed. #Deploy

---

116

The importance of the transition plan is that it gives the business leaders a roadmap to realize the change their business needs to go through. It maps out all the details that the team needs to #Deploy.

117

If business leaders don't have a plan for where they want their business to go, they will fail. Having a plan will ensure a successful business transition. #Deploy

_____

_____

_____

118

If business leaders know where their business is going, they will be able to focus and zero in on that path to get there. This is crucial in any kind of world. When it is rapidly changing, it is essential. #Deploy

_____

_____

_____

119

Involving the community in the execution of a transition plan develops their loyalty to the business. They see that the business is transitioning for them and on their behalf. #Deploy

_____

_____

_____

120

Business leaders need to ask themselves, 'What are the things of value to their community?' This question is an important guide in the transition plan because they're going to realize this plan for their community. #Deploy

_____

_____

_____

121

Business leaders can benefit from asking their community involved if the transition plan is doable. The community can provide valuable insights to iterate on the plan. #Deploy

_____

_____

_____

122

Business leaders should not be afraid to ask their community for help. Asking for help is not a weakness. It's a strength because the community wants you to succeed and will benefit. #Deploy

_____

_____

_____

123

Customers are part of the holistic community of a business. They can help business leaders make the business transition a reality. #Deploy

_____

_____

_____

124

Business leaders need to ask if their team can #Deploy the transition plan. They need to be honest with themselves when asking this question.

_____

_____

_____

125

There may be multiple routes to get to a desired destination. The fact is, one of them is the most efficient way to #Deploy a transition plan. How can you find the most efficient route to your destination?

_____

_____

_____

126

In a world of constant change, staying on the chosen route requires discipline and grit. The reward for sticking with the transition plan is huge for the business! #Deploy

_____

_____

_____

127

In a rapidly changing world, the #Transition of business leaders is a journey from where they are to where they are going. A transition plan serves as a tool to guide them through the chosen route to their destination.

_____

_____

_____

128

A route is not the be-all and end-all of a #Transition plan. It is simply a pathway leading to the desired future state of the business. What route are you going to take?

_____

_____

_____

Share the AHA messages from this book socially by going to
https://aha.pub/SlapInTheFace.

Scan the QR code or use this link to watch the section videos and more on this section topic:
https://aha.pub/SlapInTheFaceSVs

Section VII

Conclusion

Business leaders have been slapped in the face by a world they thought they knew and has likely changed forever. But it is not done. It will be changing again. We are scrambling to understand the new and become more resilient to change. But the answer is not to change and be done. The answer is to keep changing.

The old rules might be replaced with new rules. Pay no attention. There are no rules. Rules are constructs, designed to 'keep you in your lane.'

Consider a restaurant. The 'rules' suggest that it is a place to sit at a table and eat food that you order. If you want to order it to go, then there are different establishments that you can go do that. This is not the case anymore.

The rules changed on a dime when restaurants already working on razor-thin margins had to reduce maximum capacity by up to 50 percent.

Restaurants now

- offer take-out and delivery
- offer loyalty cards
- partner with local wine ships to offer perfectly paired food and wine
- offer pick-up services to bring you from home to their restaurant
- display local art for sale
- cater dinners and parties at residences

There is no limit to the possibilities once you understand what your core strengths are and what your customers are buying. (It might not be your cuisine.)

If I am a taxi driver, why can't I pick up and deliver packages as well as people? (You can.)

If I am a winery and nobody is visiting me, why can't I provide virtual tastings? (You can.)

If I am a book shop, why can't I rent books, not just sell them? (Can't you?)

Revalidate everything that you have learned in your life and about your business—*everything*.

Leaders need to focus on their value, which in turn, will deliver the results they need.

In the new contract, People First is the key and value is the lock, and by putting them together, your success metrics move up as 'work' becomes secondary and the results are everybody's business.

A business leader under the old contract might measure their staff's worth according to their wage. The new contract shows what is important to that staff member. If they can do more hours in fewer days, they save themselves *total* time, so by skipping one or more days of work, they are still paid via hours worked (so there's no additional cost to the business), but the value to the team member is priceless. Who else is going to do that for them? That staff member feels like they have a stake in the business.

The unseen value here is that people are now realizing that they are moving into the future of income, not work. The future of work was old contract thinking. The future of income is new contract thinking.

There is an urgency for businesses to change. Value is the new currency. By understanding what brings value to their community, leaders will know how to shape their businesses so they serve more people.

A new world provides an opportunity for business leaders to seize the moment. Succeeding in our new world is not a faraway dream. The moment to transition is right now!

129

Business leaders have been slapped in the face by a world they thought they knew. They are scrambling to understand the rules of our new world. They need to change fast or their businesses will cease to exist.

#Transition

_____

_____

_____

130

There is an urgency for businesses to change. Business leaders should not wait. They should ask for help from their community to understand what the market values today. #Transition

_____

_____

_____

131

Business leaders need to forget everything they think they know about business. They need to revalidate everything they have learned. Their business needs to change to succeed in this new world. #Transition

_____

_____

_____

132

Value is a new currency. By understanding what brings value to their community, business leaders will know how to shape their businesses so they serve more people. #Transition

_____

_____

_____

133

The community is essential to every stage as a business #Transitions forward. Business leaders should not try to do this by themselves. How can you involve your community in your transition plan?

_____

_____

_____

134

Transparency and honesty toward one's community is essential for business leaders in #Transition. It is the community that will keep the business on the straight path in the journey toward its desired future state.

_____

_____

_____

135

There is no limit to the #Possibilities once you understand what your core strengths are and what your customers are buying.

_____

_____

_____

136

Business owners in #Transition need to be open to receiving feedback from their community. It is keeping that transparency all the way through this journey that will set their business up for success in a world that is in constant change.

_____

_____

_____

137

Business leaders need to ask themselves and their community what the current and desired future states of their businesses are. Only then can they start mapping out all possible routes to get there. #Transition

_____

_____

_____

138

A new world provides an opportunity for business leaders to seize the moment. They should turn their focus to something that they love to do. They should be living to work and not working to live. #Transition

_____

_____

_____

139

Succeeding in our new world is not a faraway dream. There are steps that business leaders can take to transition with the change. It just takes setting up and realizing their #Transition plan.

_____

_____

_____

140

Business leaders have been slapped in the face by a world they thought they knew. They need to change for their businesses to survive and thrive in our new world. They should not wait. The moment to #Transition is now!

_____

_____

_____

Appendix 1

Sarkar's Law of Social Cycle

Indian philosopher Prabhat Ranjan Sarkar developed a theory in the 1950s that became known as 'Sarkar's Law of Social Cycle,' which in turn, contributed to what became the PROUT Institute.

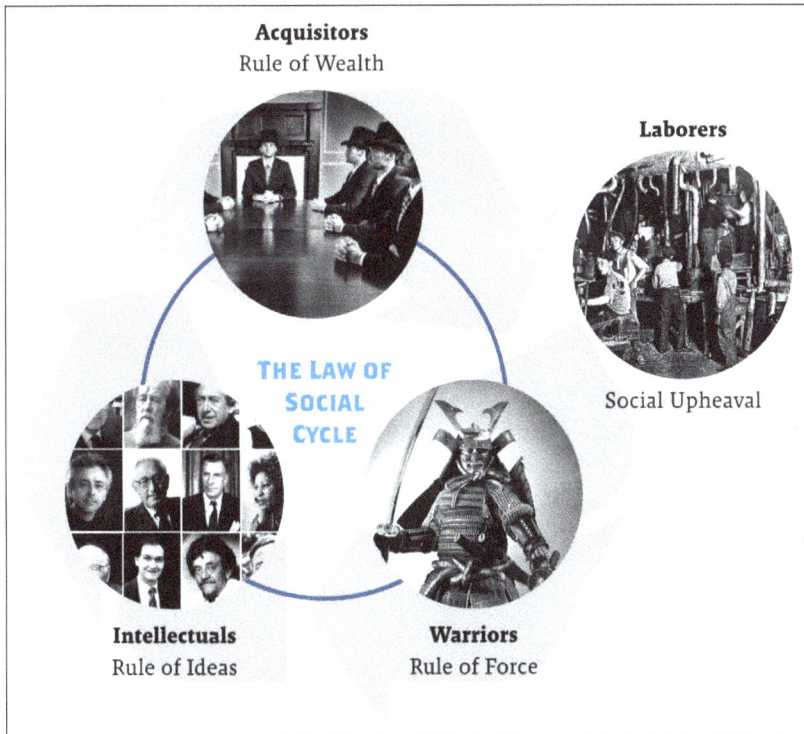

Sarkar saw the world moving through three distinct phases. In each phase, a dominant order rises to the top: acquisitors lead to warriors, warriors lead to intellectuals, intellectuals lead to acquisitors, all in a giant cycle of repetition. The graphic speaks for itself, and I will leave it to the reader to come to their own conclusions as to where they think the world was, is now, and where it is going. I can't argue with the logic, but I was constantly drawn to the fourth group: laborers, or 'Shudra,' as Sarkar called them.

"Shudra are altogether different from the first three groups. Laborers lack the energy and vigor of the warriors, the keen intellect of the intellectuals, or the ambition and drive of the accumulators. In spite of the fact that their contribution to society is profound—in fact, society could not function without them—the other groups generally look down upon and tend to exploit them. The laborers are the peasants, serfs, clerks, short-order cooks, waiters, janitors, doormen, cabdrivers, garbage collectors, truck drivers, night watchmen and factory workers who keep society running smoothly by working diligently and without complaint."

Prabhat Ranjan Sarkar

He was writing at a different time and his style is terse, but his meaning is clear and arguably even more relevant now than seventy years ago.

The twenty-first century sees that group expanded, to include bank tellers, shop assistants, cashiers, drivers, dental hygienists, caregivers, teachers, nurses, social workers, executive assistants—the list really is endless. It is that group that sits outside of what we have all come to call the '1%', as they are sometimes called. Even a senior manager working in a large company with a hefty, regular paycheck and bonuses is still someone whose time is not their own, whose 'direction' comes from others, and who must operate strictly 'in their lane'. Yes, they are practiced in the art of climbing the 'ladder to the top', but they are still not part of the '1%'.

These are the people who make the world go round. We have been trained to be the cogs in the machine. We work faster, harder, and longer, and over time, we have nearly lost ourselves to the 'service of business' with a resultant need to seek 'Work-Life Balance'. Sarkar saw it clearly. Those people were not included in his social cycle—but he knew that it was time to change.

"Humanity now needs a paradigm of development that places economic power in the hands of people."

PROUT Institute

Appendix 2

The Four Forces of Humanity

Venkatesh Rao and his writings at Ribbonfarm provided further foundations to People First thinking.

Before I explain, a quick physics refresher: science recognizes that there are four natural fundamental forces: gravitational and electromagnetic[1] and 'the strong force' and 'the weak force.'[2]

It is possible to map these forces onto a two-by-two grid, where the x axis is the measure of effect of the force and the y axis is the range of the force, which in turn, is one measure of how easy or hard it is to feel that force.

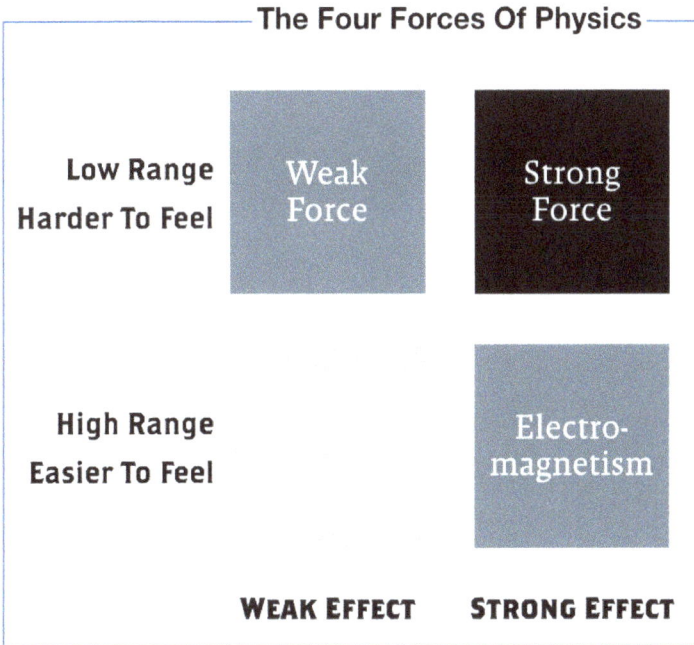

The Four Forces Of Physics

	WEAK EFFECT	STRONG EFFECT
Low Range / Harder To Feel	Weak Force	Strong Force
High Range / Easier To Feel		Electro-magnetism

---

[1]Gravitational and electromagnetic interactions produce significant long-range observable effects in everyday life.
[2]Strong and weak interactions produce forces at minuscule, subatomic distances and govern nuclear interactions.

Venkatesh re-imagined this thinking and applied it to the human condition. In his model, he saw the world comprising four fundamental forces of humanity: culture, politics, war, and business. He further argued that this order is roughly the order of decreasing strength, increasing legibility and partial subsumption of the four forces.

He used a different visualization, and I slightly modified the four forces by replacing 'war' with 'conflict'.

The '4 Forces of Humanity'—business conflict, politics, and culture—impact all of us all of the time, regardless of whether you think about them. But their impact and effect, just like the four forces of physics, can be mapped.

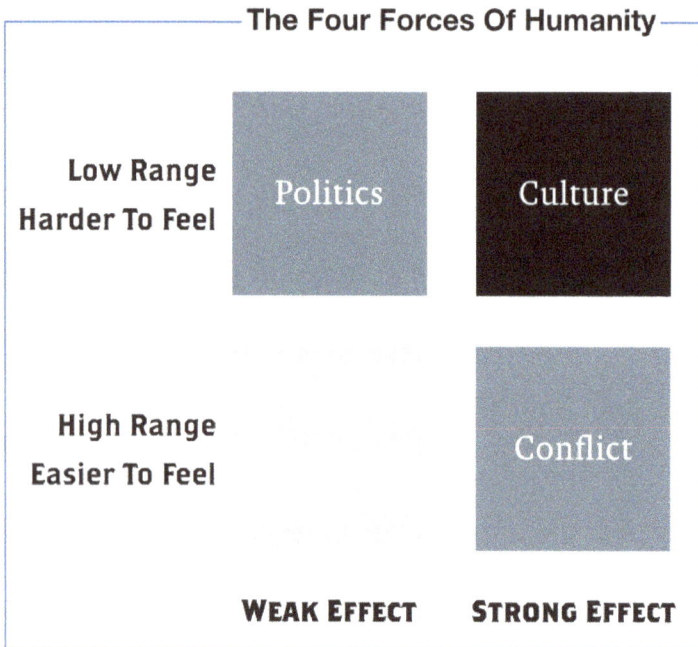

The Four Forces Of Humanity

	WEAK EFFECT	STRONG EFFECT
Low Range / Harder To Feel	Politics	Culture
High Range / Easier To Feel		Conflict

At a stroke, People First comes into sharp focus.

You can't ignore any of the forces of the natural world in your day-to-day life, but you also don't spend time thinking about why a chair is not floating above the ground or why the balloon from last night's party is stubbornly stuck to wall—neither floating up to the ceiling as a balloon should do nor sinking to the ground as it would if it had insufficient air.

Similar are the forces of humanity. You can't ignore them, but you also don't spend inordinate amounts of time pondering them. The focus of this book is on one of those four forces: business. It impacts us all in one way or another, albeit less than the forces of conflict or culture.

There is also one important difference between the four fundamental natural forces and the four human forces:

Natural forces are givens. Human forces are not.

Human forces are constructs that were created and over many years, developed by humans. If we created them, we can change them. If something isn't working, we can change it. There is nothing, absolutely nothing, that is a given, particularly in business. Business is constantly changing.

Because it is constantly changing, what we experience and feel today can change in the future. Arguably, it should—but that depends on you.

About the Author

John Philpin is a board-level executive with extensive international experience in the global software and technology industry. He specializes in the parts of business that engage with customers and has a passion for taking companies and product solutions to the global market. He is equally effective in mature established companies and fast-growth start-up environments.

John has worked with companies as diverse as GEC, Raytheon, Oracle, and Citicorp and with customers like BT, Rolls Royce, Nestlé, Chiron, HP, Johnson and Johnson, American General, and Government. He has led multi-disciplinary teams and built and taken to market software solutions that have led to contracts that have added hundreds of millions of dollars to revenue. His secret to success has always been to put people first, which is his favorite focus when presenting on topics as diverse as 'The Future of Work,' 'Identity Is Not Just ID,' 'Technology Adoption,' 'Value,' and 'Language.'

John runs his own consulting firm and advises companies, institutions, and boards.

.

.

AHAthat®

THiNKaha has created AHAthat for you to share content from this book.

- ➲ Share each AHA message socially: **https://aha.pub/SlapInTheFace**
- ➲ Share additional content: https://AHAthat.com
- ➲ Info on authoring: https://AHAthat.com/Author

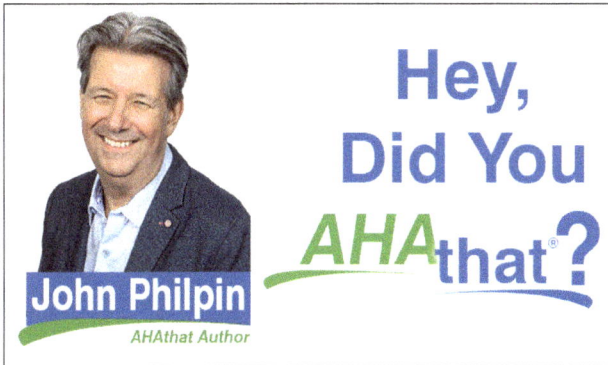

Hey,
Did You
AHAthat®?

John Philpin
AHAthat Author

www.ingramcontent.com/pod-product-compliance
Lightning Source LLC
Chambersburg PA
CBHW042118190326
41519CB00030B/7535